ALLIGATORS AND CROCODILES FUN FACTS FOR KIDS

SPEEDY
PUBLISHING

Speedy Publishing LLC
40 E. Main St. #1156
Newark, DE 19711
www.speedypublishing.com

Alligators and Crocodiles have been living on Earth for millions of years and are sometimes described as 'living fossils'.

Alligators and crocodiles are reptiles. This means they are cold-blooded and have to regulate their body temperature with their surroundings.

You can tell alligators and crocodiles apart mostly by the width of their snout. An Alligator will have a wide, broad nose while a crocodile will usually have a narrow nose.

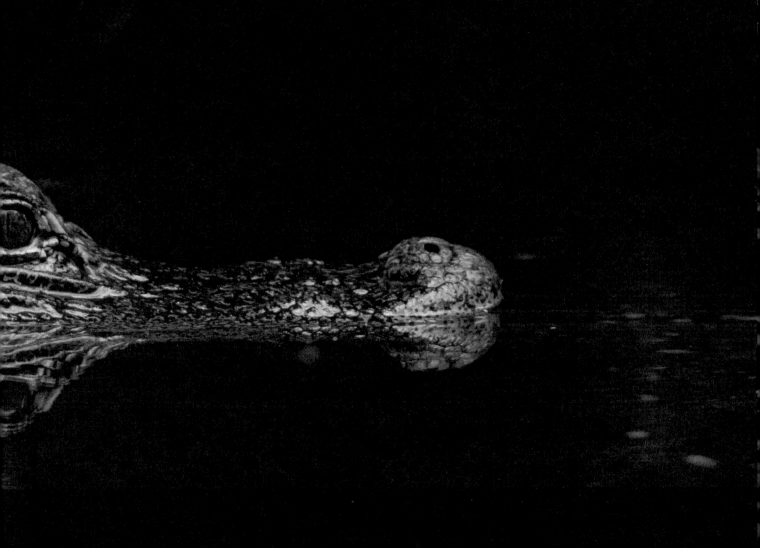

There are two different species of alligator, the American alligator and the Chinese alligator.

American alligators live in south-eastern areas of the United States such as Florida and Louisiana. Chinese alligators are found in the Yangtze River.

Crocodiles are found in the tropical habitats of Africa, Asia, Australia and the Americas. They normally live near lakes, rivers, wetlands and even some saltwater regions.

Crocodiles have the strongest bite
of any animal in the world.

Crocodiles can be often seen with their jaws wide open. They open their jaws to cool themselves because they don't have sweat glands.

45701553R00020

Made in the USA
Middletown, DE
11 July 2017